Alphabets &
Numbers

Patrick Spielman &
Sherri Spielman Valitchka

STERLING PUBLISHING CO., INC.
NEW YORK

Library of Congress Cataloging-in-Publication Data

Spielman, Patrick E.
    Alphabets & number patterns / by Patrick Spielman and Sherri
Spielman Valitchka.
        p.   cm. —(Woodworker's pattern library series)
    Includes index.
    ISBN 0-8069-0487-9
    1. Jig saws.   2. Woodwork—Patterns.   3. Lettering.   4. Numbers in
art.   5. Signs and signboards—Lettering.   I. Valitchka, Sherri
Spielman.   II. Title.   III. Title: Alphabets and number patterns.
IV. Series.
TT186.S663   1994
745.51—dc20   93-48072
Edited by Rodman Neumann   CIP

10   9   8   7   6   5

Published by Sterling Publishing Company, Inc.
387 Park Avenue South, New York, N.Y. 10016
© 1994 by Patrick Spielman & Sherri Spielman Valitchka
Distributed in Canada by Sterling Publishing
% Canadian Manda Group, P.O. Box 920, Station U
Toronto, Ontario, Canada M8Z 5P9
Distributed in Great Britain and Europe by Cassell PLC
Villiers House, 41/47 Strand, London WC2N 5JE, England
Distributed in Australia by Capricorn Link (Australia) Pty Ltd.
P.O. Box 6651, Baulkman Hills, Business Centre, NSW 2153, Australia
Manufactured in the United States of America
All rights reserved

Sterling ISBN 0-8069-0487-9

Contents

Metric Conversion

		Inches to Millimetres and Centimetres			
		MM—millimetres		CM—centimetres	
Inches	**MM**	**CM**	**Inches**	**CM**	**Inches**	**CM**

Inches	MM	CM	Inches	CM	Inches	CM
⅛	3	0.3	9	22.9	30	76.2
¼	6	0.6	10	25.4	31	78.7
⅜	10	1.0	11	27.9	32	81.3
½	13	1.3	12	30.5	33	83.8
⅝	16	1.6	13	33.0	34	86.4
¾	19	1.9	14	35.6	35	88.9
⅞	22	2.2	15	38.1	36	91.4
1	25	2.5	16	40.6	37	94.0
1¼	32	3.2	17	43.2	38	96.5
1½	38	3.8	18	45.7	39	99.1
1¾	44	4.4	19	48.3	40	101.6
2	51	5.1	20	50.8	41	104.1
2½	64	6.4	21	53.3	42	106.7
3	76	7.6	22	55.9	43	109.2
3½	89	8.9	23	58.4	44	111.8
4	102	10.2	24	61.0	45	114.3
4½	114	11.4	25	63.5	46	116.8
5	127	12.7	26	66.0	47	119.4
6	152	15.2	27	68.6	48	121.9
7	178	17.8	28	71.1	49	124.5
8	203	20.3	29	73.7	50	127.0

Preface

This book is a volume of selected letter and number patterns for woodworkers. It features various decorative alphabet designs as well as a variety of basic block script and italic letter and number styles. There are over 40 different alphabets. Most are given in both uppercase and lowercase along with matching number patterns.

One of the most popular lettering styles is the Bold Cooper, beginning on page 12. This is perhaps the most widely used style in all of the various areas of woodcrafts. Therefore, we have included this entire alphabet in three popular, ready-to-trace sizes, which in many cases will eliminate the need to enlarge or reduce the patterns.

All of the other patterns are approximately one inch high, which is suitable for making desk name signs and similar small signage. Solid-wood desk name sign blanks, pen and funnel sets, key-chain hardwares, and templates are available from various local and mail-order craft-supply outlets.

Any of the patterns in this book can be enlarged (or reduced) to whatever size may be desired. We have also included a few pattern pages of various design elements that can be incorporated to add decorative flourishes to complement your lettering or sign designs.

We encourage you to get the most out of these patterns by considering all of their possibilities for use. In addition to the variety of options cre-

The freeflowing profiles of this Bold Cooper lettering style are easy for woodworkers to reproduce with a scroll saw or router. The shapes are "forgiving" if not cut perfectly to their outlines.

Examples of letters connected to each other for freestanding use. Above, letters connect with an integral base design, whereas the foreground shows how the letter patterns of the script style from pages 44 and 45 link to each other.

Spray-on finishes that simulate stone, including granite and other hard surface materials, are available. Note the use of this finish on the letter "B" shown on the cover.

A wall clock can be personalized by routing circular bead cuts into a board and scroll-sawing the letters around the perimeter.

ated when you enlarge or reduce the patterns, you can apply them to the various crafts of woodworking in a number of ways. First, you have a wide range of materials to choose from, including solid woods, plywoods, and various plastic- and metal-overlaid sheet materials. Additionally there is a variety of natural and pigmented finishes available to get just the color or effect you want.

When these materials choices are used in conjunction with the different methods or techniques that can be utilized to actually fabricate or fashion the lettering, the possibilities are multiplied dramatically.

Individual letters and numbers can be sawn out with a scroll saw from thin or thick material. They can be made into words or names that are connected to an integral base or designed to be freestanding.

The edges of enlarged individual letters and numbers can be shaped with a router using any one of a wide variety of forming bits that are available.

Individual letters and/or numbers can be applied directly to flat backing surfaces. They can also be made to "stand off" the surface by installing small spacers behind each character.

Two letter-routing techniques were utilized to make this sign. The "Welcome to" is incised or engraved—routing with the letters cut into the surface. "Door County" is raised in relief with the surrounding background routed away.

Lettering can be raised in relief by sandblasting away the background.

Letters and numbers can be hand- or router-carved so that they stand in relief above the background or are incised—carved into the surface. The same relief or incised results can be achieved using the popular technique of sandblasting.

The books *Making Wood Signs*, *Scroll Saw Basics*, and *The New Router Handbook* are suggested references for individuals needing more information about various techniques. Refer to page 125.

Patrick Spielman and
Sherri Spielman Valitchka

Basic Tips

The patterns and project ideas in this book are essentially fast, easy, and fun to create. Making these cutouts requires no special equipment other than a scroll saw and a drill to make holes for sawing inside openings. Advanced woodworking skills are not required.

Sizing Patterns with a Photocopier

Most communities have photocopiers available with enlarging capabilities; they're found in public libraries, banks, and schools. Print shops and specialized businesses ("copy shops") are found in most areas. Check the business index of your telephone directory under the headings "photo-

copying" or "copying" for the nearest business specializing in this service. Having a copy made is quick, convenient, and far more expedient and accurate than other old-fashioned ways of copying or enlarging patterns that used the squared grid system or pantograph tracings.

Enlarging with a Proportional Scale

Better-quality photocopiers enlarge or reduce pattern sizes in one-percent increments. Typically, they can enlarge up to 200 percent of the original where the original is referred to as 100 percent. A proportional scale is an inexpensive circular device that allows you to determine the exact percentage of enlargement or reduction needed to produce a specific-sized pattern. The photocopier is then set to that percentage. The scale is very easy to use; all the little numbers and divisions make it look much more complicated to use than it really is. This device is simply two rotating discs with numbers and scale divisions around their perimeters, joined by a common pivot. Align the number or dimension you have on the inner disc with the dimension you want on the outer disc. The exact percentage to set the copy machine can then be read in the opening directly below the arrow.

To see how helpful this tool is, and how easy it actually is to use, follow the steps illustrated here which show a typical enlargement application. This process eliminates the guesswork and trial-and-error methods from the sizing process. This method also saves paper and money spent on wasted copies. Proportional scales are found in art, graphics, and printing-supply stores. Check the business section of your telephone directory to locate a source for one of these helpful devices.

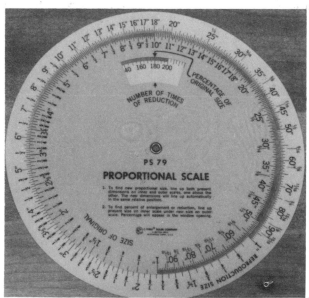

An inexpensive proportional scale such as this makes enlarging or reducing patterns to a specific size with a photocopy machine quick and precise.

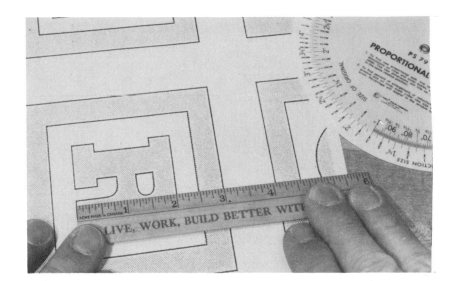

Here's a typical problem example: the objective is to enlarge this two-inch-high letter to 3½ inches.

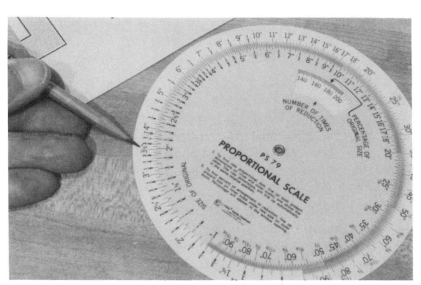

Simply line up the two-inch mark of the inner disc to the 3½-inch mark on the outer disc. Now read the exact percentage required to set the copy machine to get an enlarged copy of the desired size. In this example you will get a 3½-inch letter when the original is enlarged 175 percent.

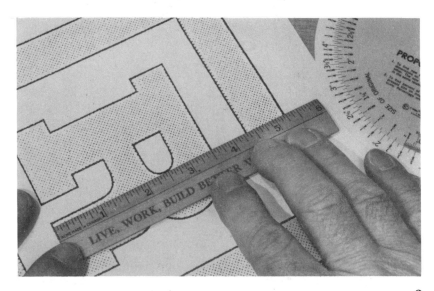

The enlarged letter pattern is exactly 3½ inches high.

Transferring Patterns to the Wood

Transferring patterns to material for sawing can certainly be done in traditional ways, such as tracing with copy papers (carbon or graphite). However, the new, faster techniques involve: (1) copying the pattern directly from the book on an office-quality copy machine, at which time it can be enlarged or reduced as desired, (2) scissor-cutting the pattern to a rough size, (3) coating the back of the pattern with a very light mist of special spray adhesive, and (4) simply hand-pressing the paper pattern copy directly onto the workpiece. Temporary bonding spray adhesives are available from craft shops and mail-order sources. One kind we use is 3-M's Scotch Brand Spray Mount Adhesive, but other brands work equally well. Some craftspeople prefer using a brush-on application of rubber cement for securing patterns to the workpiece.

Test the adhesive on scrap first, before using. To use the spray adhesive, simply spray a very light mist onto the back of the pattern copy—do not spray it on the wood. Wait 10–30 seconds, and press the pattern onto the workpiece. It should maintain contact during sawing. After all the cutting is completed, the paper pattern should peel very easily and cleanly from the workpiece without effort. Should the pattern be difficult to remove because too much adhesive was used, simply wipe the top of the pattern with rag that has been slightly dampened in solvent.

Apply a very light "mist" of spray adhesive only to the back of the pattern. Do not spray directly onto the wood. Note that a newspaper underneath the pattern is being used to catch the overspray.

A pattern has been applied to the wood, and it is ready for sawing. Use a temporary-mounting type of spray adhesive as shown or rubber cement. Both allow for easy removal of the pattern after sawing is complete.

Making Trace-Around Templates

Professional wood sign makers who lay out work for hand and router carving, sandblasting, or scroll sawing often have good use for clear plastic templates of a particular style and size of alphabet. It is a fairly straightforward process to make your own trace-around (and/or router-guiding) transparent plastic templates with a scroll saw. Simply enlarge or reduce the alphabet/number characters to the size that is desired. Lay out a continuous alphabet onto the protective surface masking of ¹⁄₁₆-inch-thick or less (¼-inch for routing templates) clear plastic (Lexan or Polycarbonate are best). Connect each letter to the next along its bottom, forming a continuous baseline strip in a manner that is similar to the layout of the name signs shown earler. Fasten the plastic to a ¼-inch scrap plywood backer using double-faced tape. Cut out the template using a No. 5 or No. 7 regular skip-tooth blade at a medium to slow speed. Discard the plywood backer, and remove the protective masking from the plastic. You have a ready-to-trace clear plastic template of your favorite alphabet or set of numbers, made in the size you require.

Letter & Number Patterns

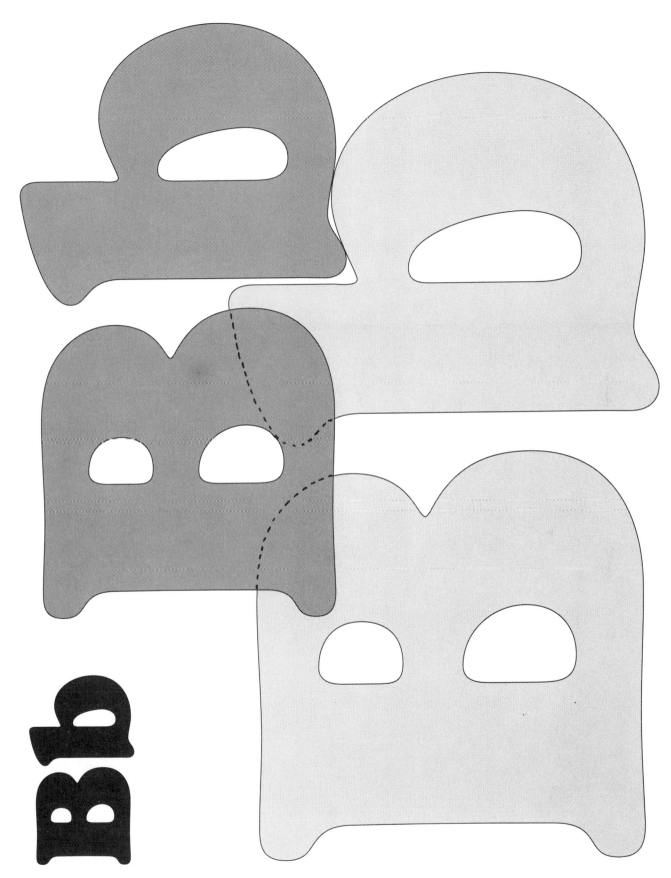

14

15

Ff

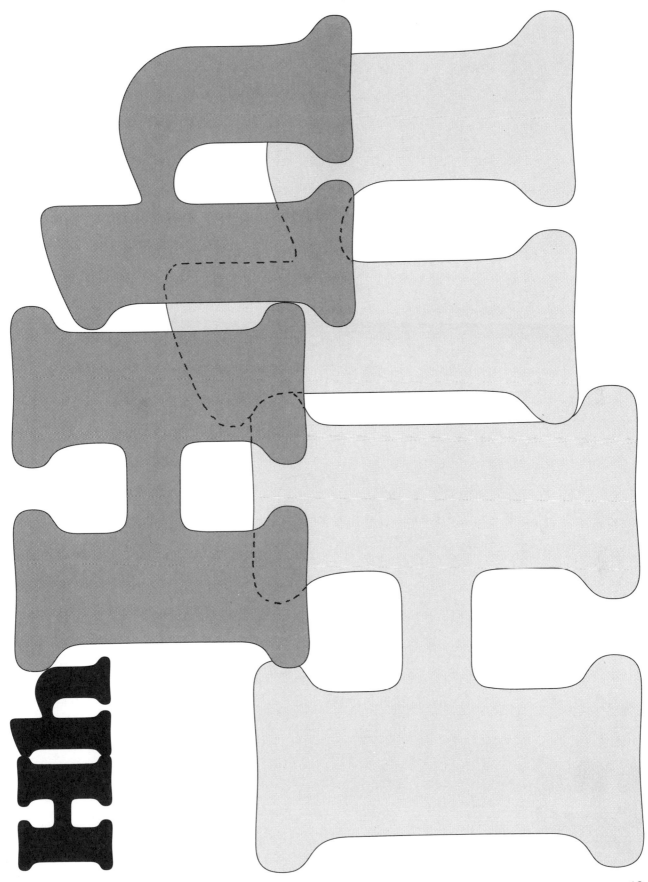

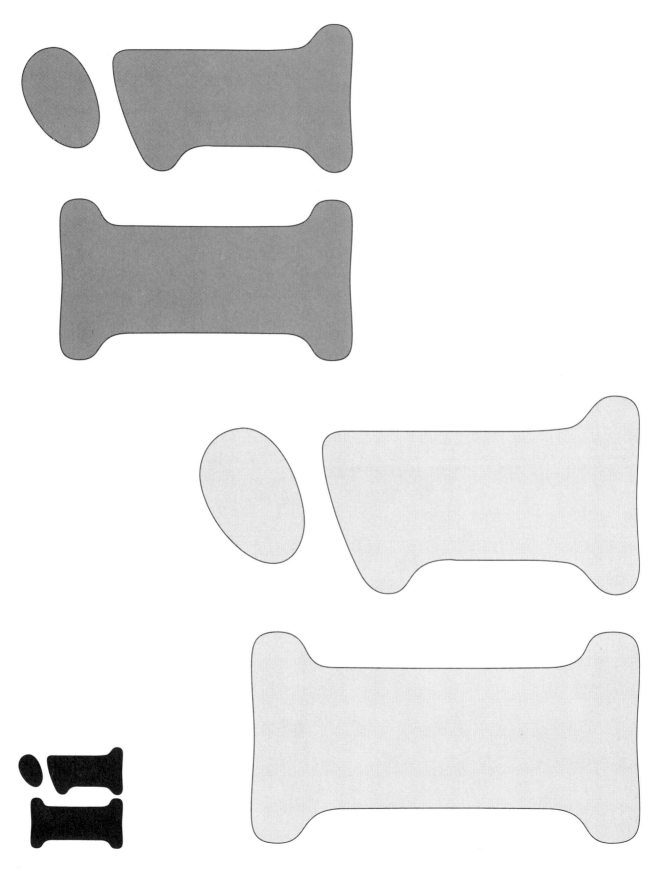

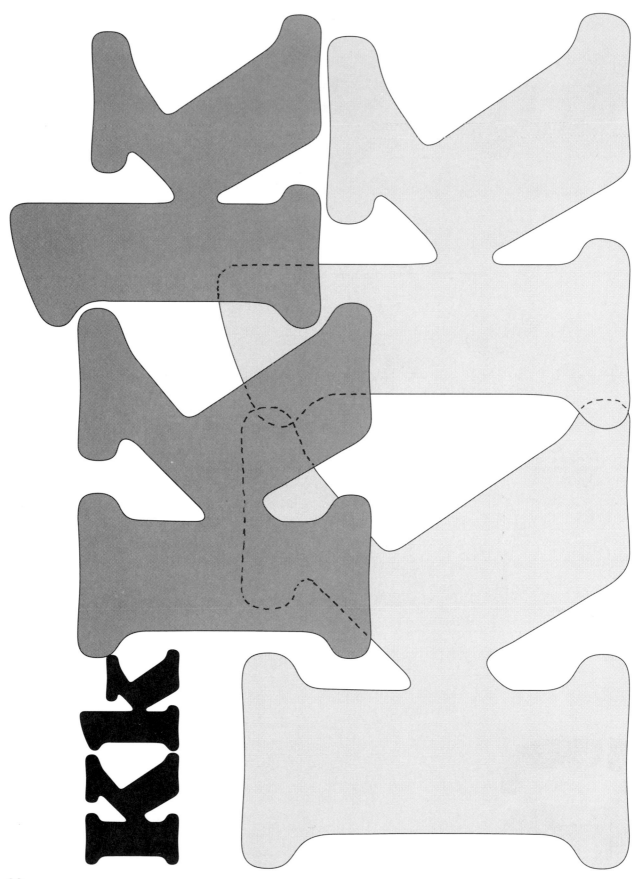

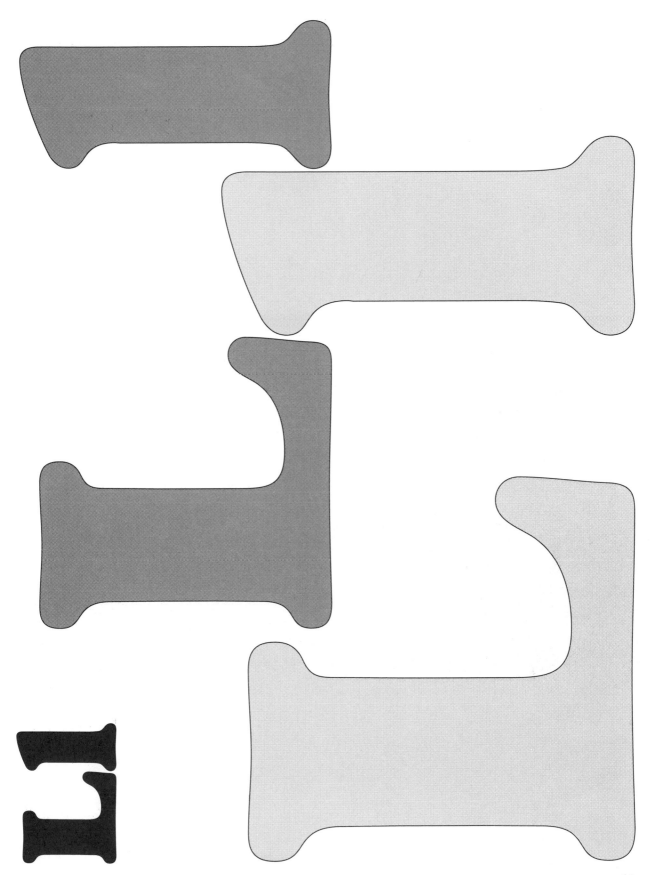

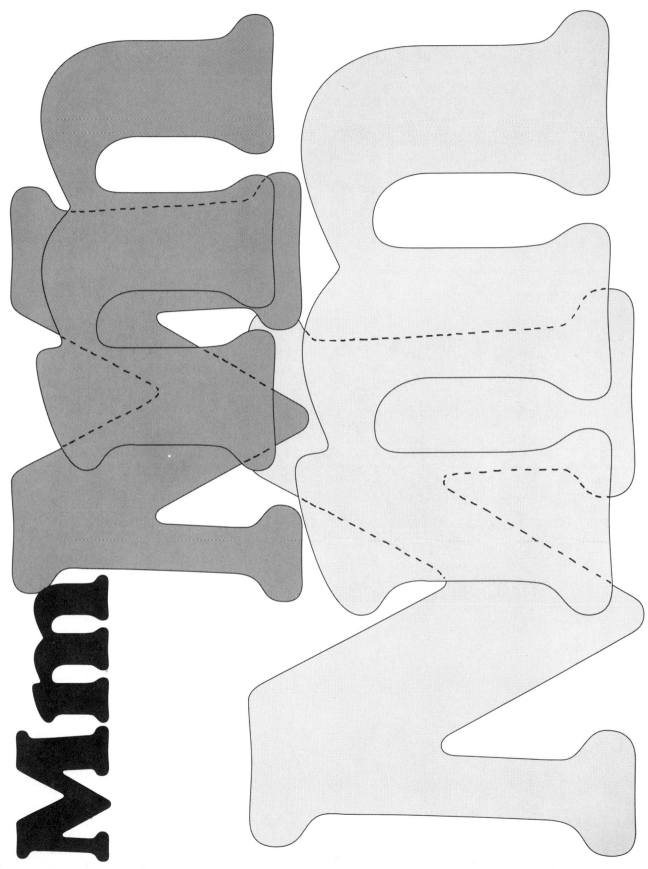

Mm

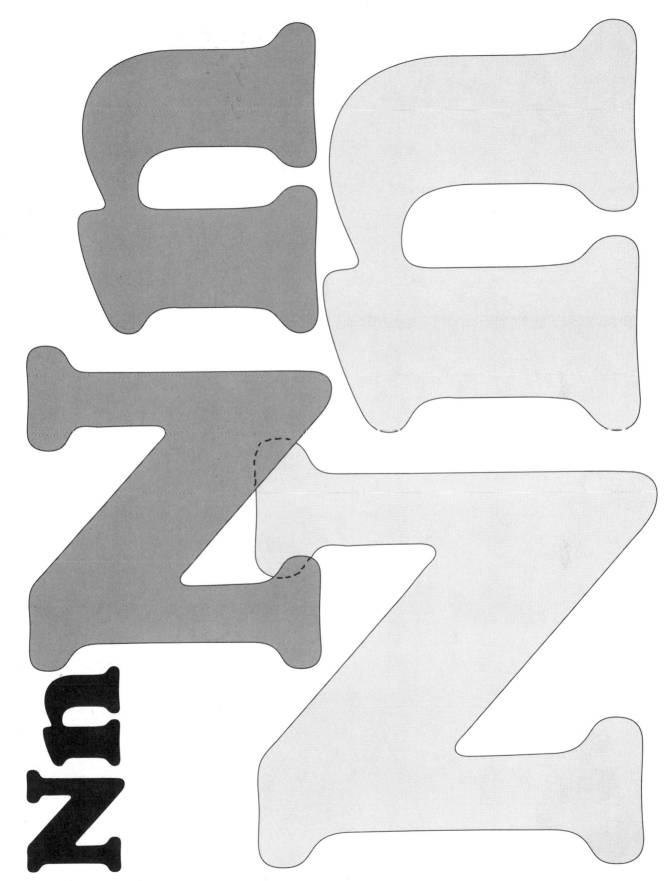

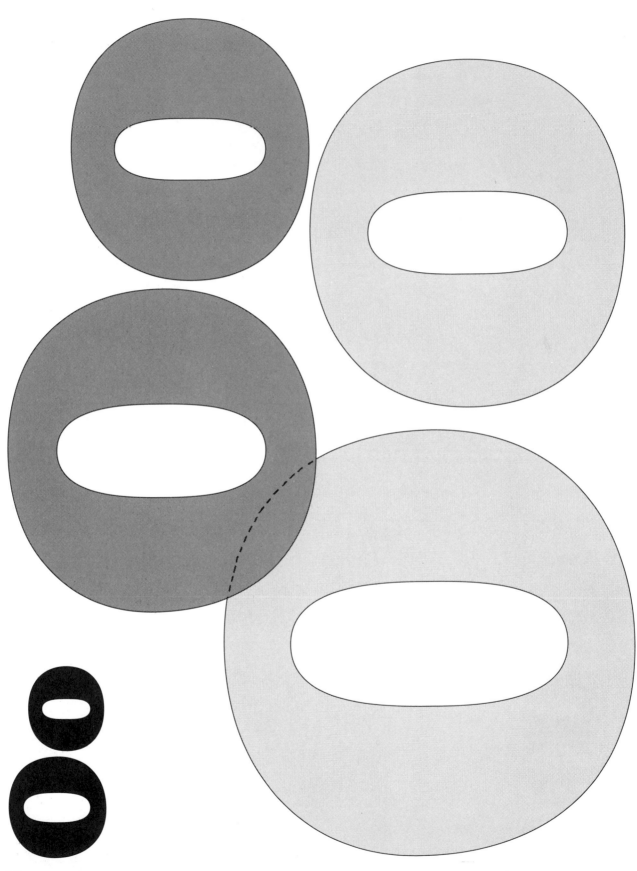

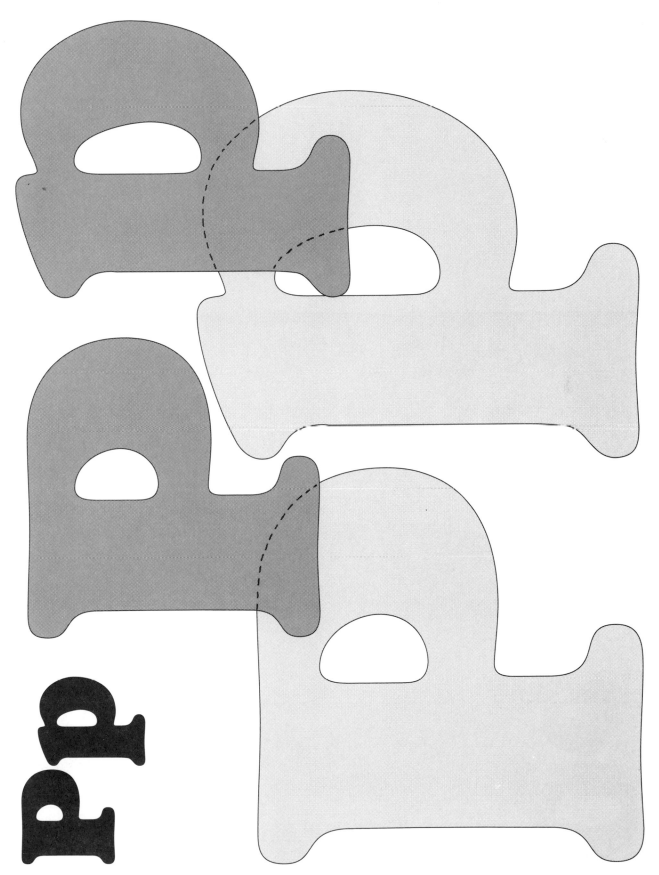

P p

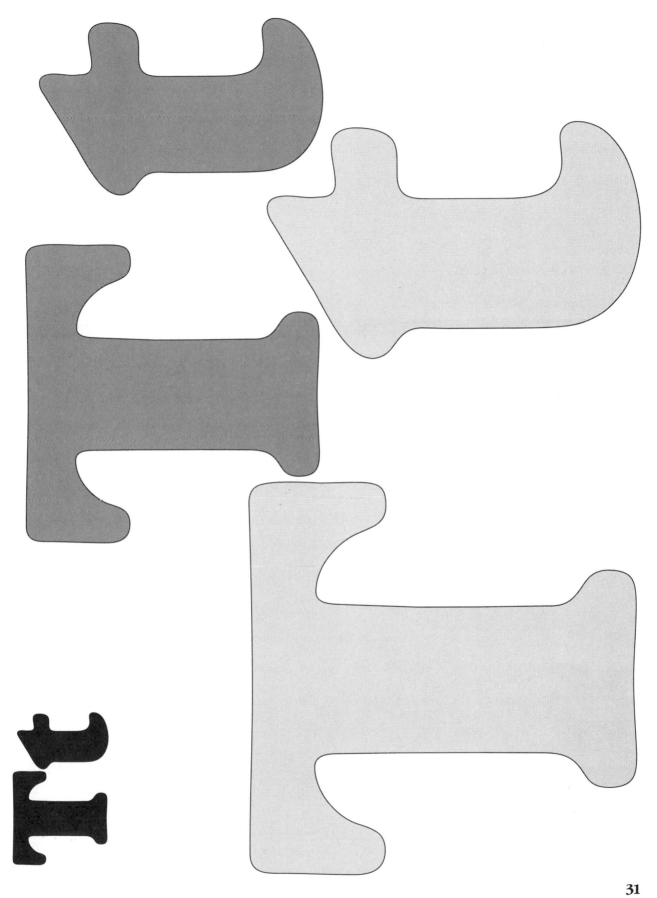

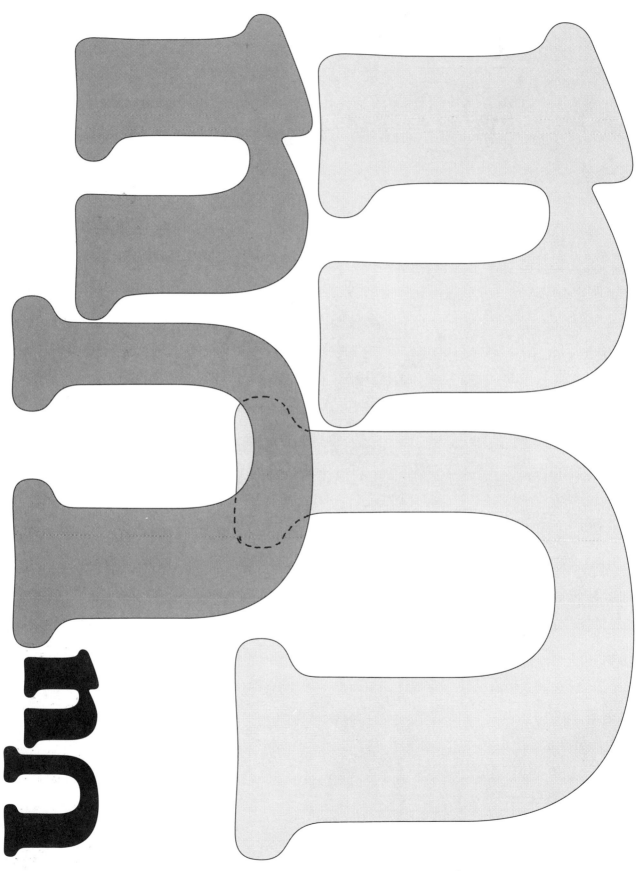

Uu

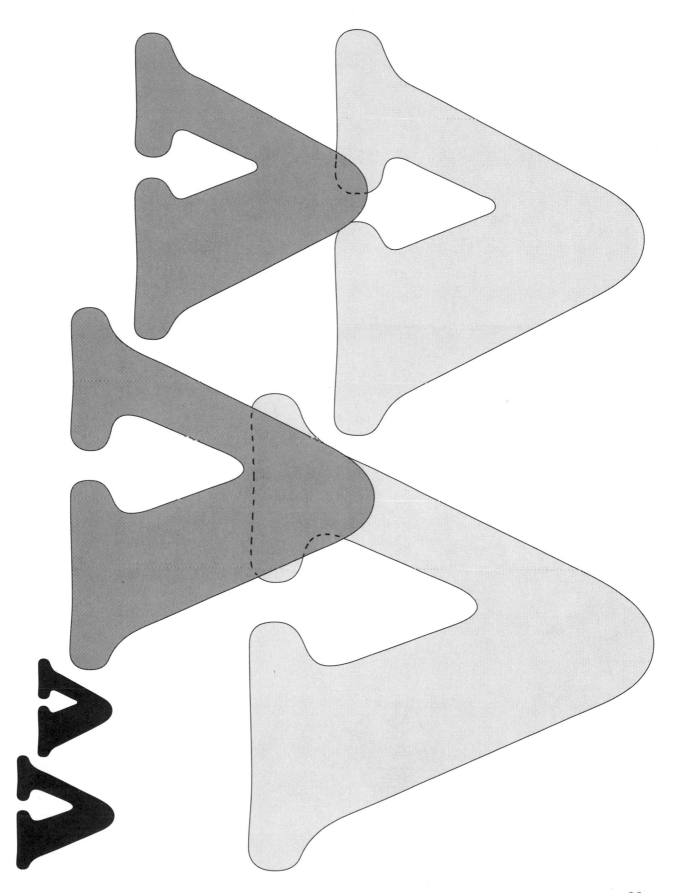

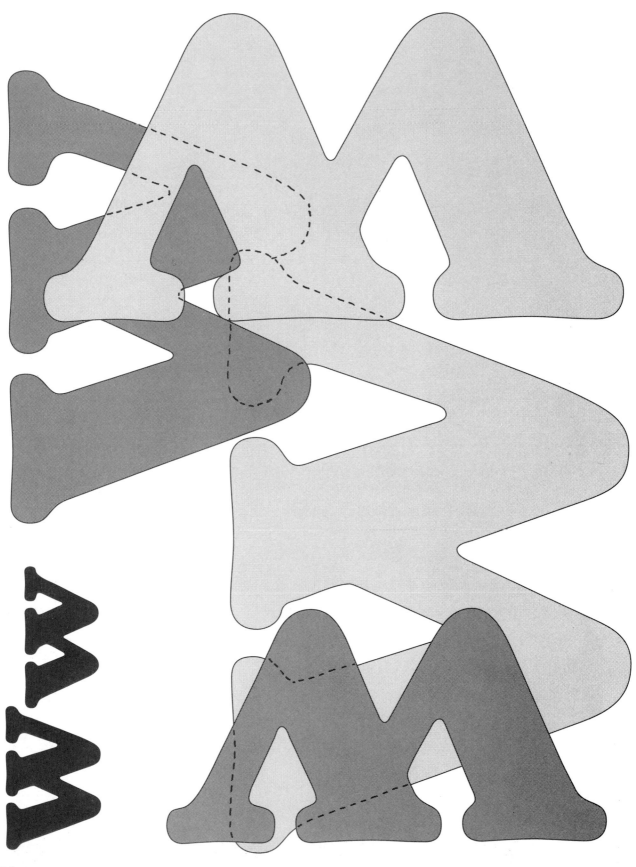

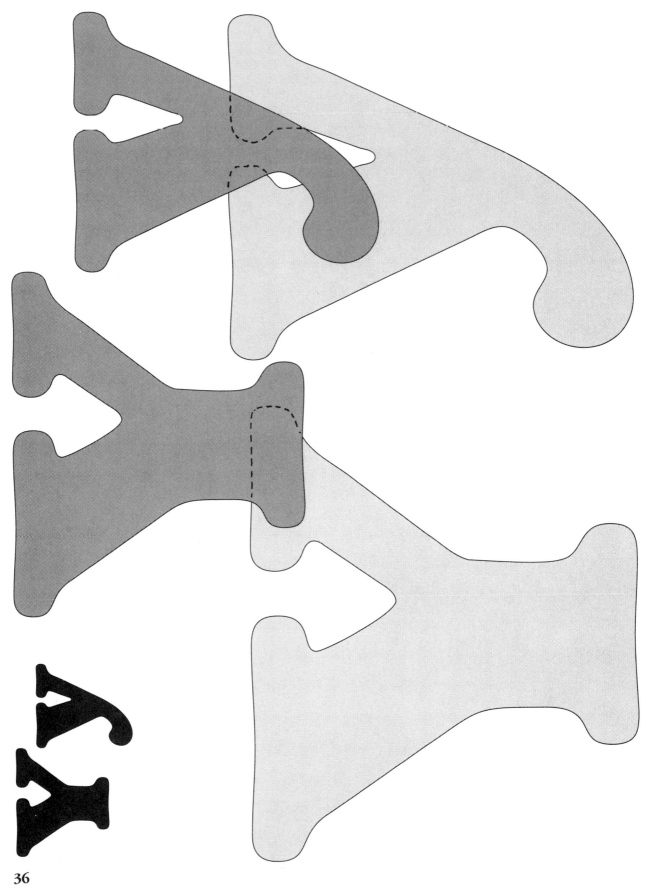

36

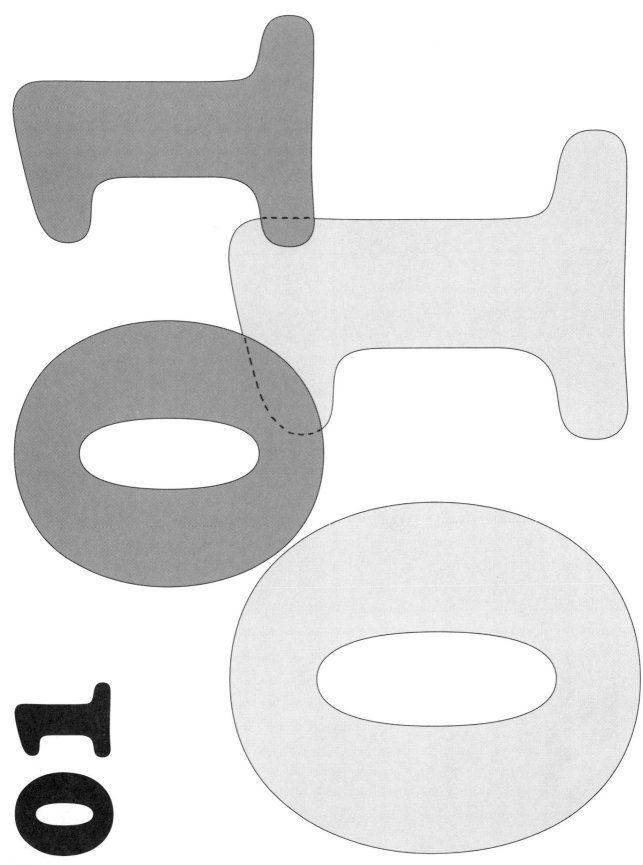

23

67

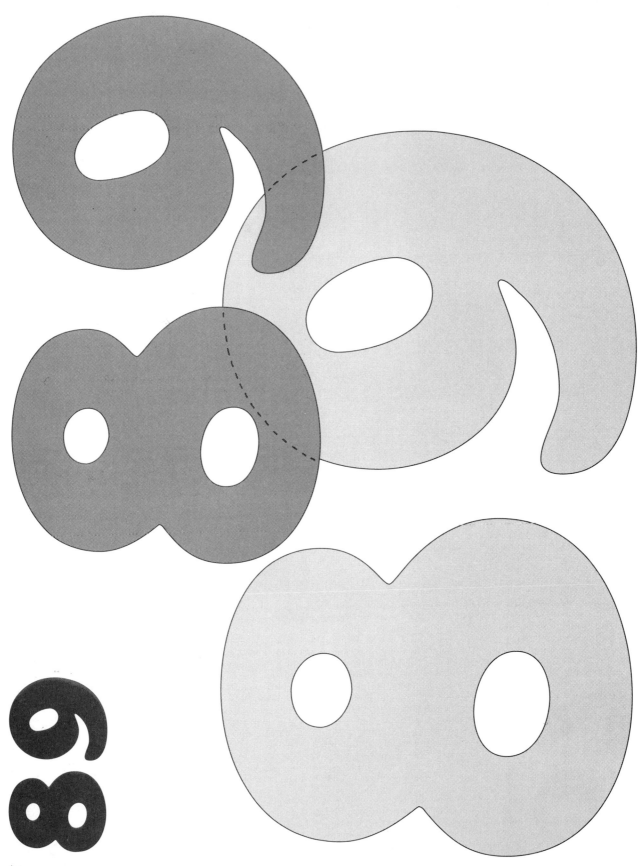

89

42

A B C D
E F G H I
J K L M
N O P Q
R S T U V
W X Y Z &

Aa Bb Cc

Dd Ee Ff

Gg Hh Ii

Jj Kk Ll

Mm Nn Oo

Pp Qq Rr

Ss Tt Uu

Vv Ww Xx

Yy Zz

0 1 2 3 4

5 6 7 8 9

& ? ! $;

Aa Bb Cc
Dd Ee Ff
Gg Hh Ii
Jj Kk Ll
Mm Nn Oo
Pp Qq Rr

Ss Tt Uu

Vv Ww Xx

Yy Zz

0 1 2 3 4

5 6 7 8 9

& ? ! $;

Aa Bb Cc
Dd Ee Ff
Gg Hh Ii
Jj Kk Ll
Mm Nn Oo
Pp Qq Rr

Ss Tt Uu

Vv Ww Xx

Yy Zz

0 1 2 3 4

5 6 7 8 9

& ? ! $;

AaBbCc

DdEeFf

GgHhIi

JjKkLl

MmNnOo

PpQqRr

SsTt Uu

VvWwXx

Yy Zz

0 1 2 3 4

5 6 7 8 9

& ? ! $;

Aa Bb Cc
Dd Ee Ff
Gg Hh Ii
Jj Kk Ll
Mm Nn Oo
Pp Qq Rr

Ss Tt Uu
Vv Ww Xx
Yy Zz
0 1 2 3 4
5 6 7 8 9
& ? ! $;

Aa Bb Cc

Dd Ee Ff

Gg Hh Ii

Jj Kk Ll

Mm Nn Oo

Pp Qq Rr

Ss Tt Uu

Vv Ww Xx

Yy Zz

0 1 2 3 4

5 6 7 8 9

& ? ! $;

Aa Bb Cc

Dd Ee Ff

Gg Hh Ii

Jj Kk Ll

Mm Nn Oo

Pp Qq Rr

Ss Tt Uu
Vv Ww Xx
Yy Zz
0 1 2 3 4
5 6 7 8 9
& ? ! $;

A B C

D E F

G H I

J K L

M N O

P Q R

STU
VW
XYZ
01234
5678
9&?!$;

Aa Bb Cc Dd Ee Ff Gg Hh Ii Jj Kk Ll MmNnOo Pp Qq Rr

Ss Tt Uu

Vv Ww Xx

Yy Zz

0 1 2 3 4

5 6 7 8 9

& ? ! $;

Aa Bb Cc
Dd Ee Ff
Gg Hh Ii
Jj Kk Ll
Mm Nn Oo
Pp Qq Rr

Ss Tt Uu
Vv Ww Xx
Yy Zz
0 1 2 3 4
5 6 7 8 9
& ? ! $;

Aa Bb Cc

Dd Ee Ff

Gg Hh Ii

Jj Kk Ll

Mm Nn Oo

Pp Qq Rr

Ss Tt Uu
Vv Ww Xx
Yy Zz
1 2 3 4
5 6 7 8
9 $ K

Aa Bb Cc
Dd Ee Ff
Gg Hh Ii
Jj Kk Ll
Mm Nn Oo
Pp Qq Rr

Ss Tt Uu

Vv Ww Xx

Yy Zz

0 1 2 3 4

5 6 7 8 9

& ? ! $;

Aa Bb Cc
Dd Ee Ff
Gg Hh Ii
Jj Kk Ll
Mm Nn Oo
Pp Qq Rr

Ss Tt Uu
Vv Ww Xx
Yy Zz
0 1 2 3 4
5 6 7 8 9
& ? ! $;

Aa Bb Cc
Dd Ee Ff
Gg Hh Ii
Jj Kk Ll
Mm Nn Oo
Pp Qq Rr

Ss Tt Uu

Vv Ww Xx

Yy Zz

0 1 2 3 4

5 6 7 8 9

& ? ! $;

Aa Bb Cc

Dd Ee Ff

Gg Hh Ii

Jj Kk Ll

Mm Nn Oo

Pp Qq Rr

Ss Tt Uu

Vv Ww Xx

Yy Zz

0 1 2 3 4

5 6 7 8 9

& ? ! $;

Aa Bb Cc
Dd Ee Ff
Gg Hh Ii
Jj Kk Ll
Mm Nn Oo
Pp Qq Rr

Ss Tt Uu
Vv Ww Xx
Yy Zz
0 1 2 3 4
5 6 7 8 9
& ? ! $;

A B C
D E F
G H I
J K L
M N O
P Q R

S T U
V W X
Y Z
0 1 2 3 4
5 6 7 8 9
& ? ! $;

A B C
D E F
G H I
J K L
M N O
P Q R

S T U
V W X
Y Z
0 1 2 3 4
5 6 7 8 9
& ? ! $;

AaBbCc
DdEeFf
GgHhIi
JjKkLl
MmNn
OoPpQq

RrSsTt
UuVvWw
XxYyZz

0 1 2 3 4

5 6 7 8 9

& ? ! $;

A B C
D E F
G H I
J K L
M N O
P Q R

S T U
V W X
Y Z
0 1 2 3 4
5 6 7 8 9
& ? ! $;

Aa Bb Cc
Dd Ee Ff
Gg Hh Ii
Jj Kk Ll
MmNn Oo
Pp Qq Rr

Ss Tt Uu
Vv WwXx
Yy Zz
0 1 2 3 4
5 6 7 8 9
& ? ! $;

Aa Bb Cc
Dd Ee Ff
Gg Hh Ii
Jj Kk Ll
Mm Nn Oo
Pp Qq Rr

Ss Tt Uu

Vv Ww Xx

Yy Zz

0 1 2 3 4

5 6 7 8 9

& ? ! $;

AaBbCc
DdEeFf
GgHhIi
JjKkLl
MmNn
OoPpQq

Rr Ss Tt

Uu Uu Ww

Xx Yy Zz

0 1 2 3 4

5 6 7 8 9

& ? ! $;

Aa Bb Cc
Dd Ee Ff
Gg Hh Ii
Jj Kk Ll
Mm Nn Oo
Pp Qq Rr

Ss Tt Uu
Vv Ww Xx
Yy Zz

0 1 2 3 4
5 6 7 8 9
& ? ! $;

Aa Bb Cc
Dd Ee Ff
Gg Hh Ii
Jj Kk Ll
Mm Nn Oo
Pp Qq Rr

Ss Tt Uu
Vv Ww Xx
Yy Zz

0 1 2 3 4
5 6 7 8 9

& ? ! $;

Aa Bb Cc
Dd Ee Ff
Gg Hh Ii
Jj Kk Ll
Mm Nn Oo
Pp Qq Rr

Ss Tt Uu

Vv Ww Xx

Yy Zz

0 1 2 3 4

5 6 7 8 9

& ? ! $;

Aa Bb Cc
Dd Ee Ff
Gg Hh Ii
Jj Kk Ll
Mm Nn Oo
Pp Qq Rr

Ss Tt Uu
Vv Ww Xx
Yy Zz

0 1 2 3 4
5 6 7 8 9
& ? ! $;

Aa Bb Cc
Dd Ee Ff
Gg Hh Ii
Jj Kk Ll
Mm Nn Oo
Pp Qq Rr

Ss Tt Uu
Vv WwXx
Yy Zz
0 1 2 3 4
5 6 7 8 9
& ? ! $;

Aa Bb Cc
Dd Ee Ff
Gg Hh Ii
Jj Kk Ll
Mm Nn Oo
Pp Qq Rr

Ss Tt Uu
Vv Ww Xx
Yy Zz
0 1 2 3 4
5 6 7 8 9
& ? ! $;

AaBbCc
DdEeFf
GgHhIi
JjKkLl
MmNn
OoPpQq

Rr Ss Tt

Uu Vv Ww

Xx Yy Zz

0 1 2 3 4

5 6 7 8 9

& ? ! $:

S s T t U u
V v W w X x
Y y Z z
0 1 2 3
4 5 6 7
8 9

Aa Bb Cc
Dd Ee Ff
Gg Hh Ii
Jj Kk Ll
Mm Nn Oo
Pp Qq Rr

Ss Tt Uu

Vv Ww Xx

Yy Zz

0 1 2 3 4

5 6 7 8 9

& ? ! $;

Aa Bb Cc
Dd Ee Ff
Gg Hh Ii
Jj Kk Ll
Mm Nn
Oo Pp Qq

Rr Ss Tt UuVvWw Xx Yy Zz

0 1 2 3 4

5 6 7 8 9

& ? ! $;

Aa Bb Cc
Dd Ee Ff
Gg Hh Ii
Jj Kk Ll
MmNnOo
Pp Qq Rr

Ss Tt Uu

Vv Ww Xx

Yy Zz

0 1 2 3 4

5 6 7 8 9

& ? ! $;

Aa Bb Cc

Dd Ee Ff

Gg Hh Ii

Jj Kk Ll

Mm Nn Oo

Pp Qq Rr

Ss   Tt   Uu

Vv   Ww   Xx

Yy   Zz

0   1   2   3   4

5   6   7   8   9

&   ?   ! $;

Aa Bb Cc
Dd Ee Ff
Gg Hh Ii
Jj Kk Ll
Mm Nn Oo
Pp Qq Rr

Ss Tt Uu

Yy Vv Ww Xx

Yy Zz

0 1 2 3 4

5 6 7 8 9

& ? ! $;

Aa Bb Cc

Dd Ee Ff

Gg Hh Ii

Jj Kk Ll

Mm Nn Oo

Pp Qq Rr

Ss Tt Uu
Vv Ww Xx
Yy Zz
0 1 2 3 4
5 6 7 8 9
& ? ! $;

Aa Bb Cc
Dd Ee Ff
Gg Hh Ii
Jj Kk Ll
Mm Nn Oo
Pp Qq Rr

Ss Tt Uu
Uu Ww Xx
Yy Zz
0 1 2 3 4
5 6 7 8 9
& ? ! $;

Decorative Accents

the Coffee Shoppe

❧ Maureen

Current Books by Patrick Spielman

Carving Wild Animals: Life-Size Wood Figures. Spielman and renowned woodcarver Bill Dehos show how to carve more than 20 magnificent creatures of the North American wilds. A cougar, black bear, prairie dog, squirrel, raccoon, and fox are some of the life-size animals included. Step-by-step, photo-filled instructions and multiple-view patterns, plus tips on the use of tools, wood election, finishing, and polishing, help bring each animal to life. Oversized. Over 300 photos. 16 pages in full color. 240 pages.

Christmas Scroll Saw Patterns. Patrick and Patricia Spielman provide over 200 original, full-size scroll-saw patterns with Christmas as the theme, including: toys; shelves; tree, window, and table decorations; segmented projects; and alphabets. A wide variety of Santas, trees, and holiday animals are included, as is a short, illustrated review of scroll-saw techniques. 4 pages in color. 164 pages.

Classic Fretwork Scroll Saw Patterns. Spielman and coauthor James Reidle provide over 140 imaginative patterns inspired by and derived from mid- to late-19th-century scroll-saw masters. This book covers nearly 30 categories of patterns and includes a brief review of scroll-saw techniques and how to work with patterns. These include ornamental numbers and letters, beautiful birds, signs, wall pockets, silhouettes, a sleigh, jewelry boxes, toy furniture, and more. 192 pages.

Country Mailboxes. Spielman and coauthor Paul Meisel have come up with the 20 best country-style mailbox designs. They include an old pump fire wagon, a Western saddle, a Dalmatian, and even a boy fishing. Simple instructions cover cutting, painting, decorating, and installation. Over 200 illustrations. 4 pages in color. 164 pages.

Gluing & Clamping. A thorough, up-to-date examination of one of the most critical steps in woodworking. Spielman explores the features of every type of glue—from traditional animal-hide glues to the newest epoxies—the clamps and tools needed, the bonding properties of different wood species, safety tips, and all techniques from edge-to-edge and end-to-end gluing to applying plastic laminates. Also included is a glossary of terms. Over 500 illustrations. 256 pages.

Making Country-Rustic Wood Projects. Hundreds of photos, patterns, and detailed scaled drawings reveal construction methods, woodworking techniques, and Spielman's professional secrets for making indoor and outdoor furniture in the distinctly attractive Country-Rustic style. Covered are all aspects of furniture making from choosing the best wood for the job to texturing smooth boards. Among the dozens of projects are mailboxes, cabinets, shelves, coffee tables, weather vanes, doors, panelling, plant stands, and many other durable and economical pieces. 400 illustrations. 4 pages in color. 164 pages.

Making Wood Bowls with a Router & Scroll Saw. Using scroll-sawn rings, inlays, fretted edges, and much more, Spielman and master craftsman Carl Roehl have developed a completely new approach to creating decorative bowls. Over 200 illustrations. 8 pages in color. 168 pages.

Making Wood Decoys. This clear, step-by-step approach to the basics of decoy carving is abundantly illustrated with close-up photos for designing, selecting, and obtaining woods; tools; feather detailing; painting; and finishing of decorative and working decoys. Six different professional decoy artists are featured. Photo gallery (4 pages in full color) along with numerous detailed plans for various popular decoys. 164 pages.

Making Wood Signs. Designing, selecting woods and tools, and every process through finishing are clearly covered. Instructions for hand and power carving, routing, and sandblasting techniques for small to huge signs. Foolproof guides for professional letters and ornaments. Hundreds of photos (4 pages in full color). Lists sources for supplies and special tooling. 148 pages.

New Router Handbook. This updated and expanded version of the definitive guide to routing continues to revolutionize router use. The text, with over 1,000 illustrations, covers familiar and new routers, bits, accessories, and tables available today; complete maintenance and safety techniques; a multitude of techniques for both hand-held and mounted routers; plus dozens of helpful shop-made fixtures and jigs. 384 pages.

Original Scroll Saw Shelf Patterns. Patrick Spielman and Loren Raty provide over 50 original, full-size patterns for wall shelves, which may be copied applied directly to wood. Photographs of finished shelves are included, as well as information on choosing woods, stack-sawing, and finishing. 4 pages in color. 132 pages.

Realistic Decoys. Spielman and master carver Keith Bridenhagen reveal their successful techniques for carving, feather-texturing, painting, and finishing wood decoys. Details you can't find elsewhere—anatomy, attitudes, markings, and the easy, step-by-step approach to perfect delicate procedures—make this book invaluable. Includes listings for contests, shows, and sources of tools and supplies. 274 close-up photos. 8 pages in color. 232 pages.

Router Basics. With over 200 close-up, step-by-step photos and drawings, this valuable starter handbook will guide the new owner, as well as provide a spark to owners for whom the router isn't the tool they turn to most often. Covers all the basic router styles, along with how-it-works descriptions of all its major features. Includes sections on bits and accessories, as well as square-cutting and trimming, case and furniture routing, cutting circles and arcs, template and freehand routing, and using the router with a router table. 128 pages.

Router Jigs & Techniques. A practical encyclopedia of information, covering the latest equipment to use with the router, it describes all the newest commercial routing machines, along with jigs, bits, and other aids and devices. The book not only provides invaluable tips on how to determine which router and bits to buy, it explains how to get the most out of the equipment once it is bought. Over 800 photos and illustrations. 384 pages.

Scroll Saw Basics. Features more than 275 illustrations covering basic techniques and accessories. Sections include types of saws, features, selection of blades, safety, and how to use patterns. Half a dozen patterns are included to help the scroll saw user get started. Basic cutting techniques are covered, including inside cuts, bevel cuts, stack-sawing, and others. 128 pages.

Scroll Saw Country Patterns. With 300 full-size patterns in 28 categories, this selection of projects covers an extraordinary range, with instructions every step of the way. Projects include farm animals, people, birds, and butterflies, plus letter and key holders, coasters, switch plates, country hearts, and more. Directions for piercing, drilling, sanding, and finishing, as well as tips on using special tools. 4 pages in color. 196 pages.

Scroll Saw Fretwork Patterns. This companion book to *Scroll Saw Fretwork Techniques & Projects* features over 200 fabulous, full-size fretwork patterns. These patterns include popular classic designs, plus an array of imaginative contemporary ones. Choose from a variety of numbers, signs, brackets, animals, miniatures, silhouettes, and more. 256 pages.

Scroll Saw Fretwork Techniques & Projects. A study in the historical development of fretwork, as well as the tools, techniques, materials, and project styles that have evolved over the past 130 years. Every intricate turn and cut is explained, with over 550 step-by-step photos and illustrations. 32 projects are shown in full color. The book also covers some modern scroll-sawing machines as well as state-of-the-art fretwork and fine scroll-sawing techniques. 8 pages in color. 232 pages.

Scroll Saw Handbook. The workshop manual to this versatile tool includes the basics (how scroll saws work, blades to use, etc.) and the advantages and disadvantages of the general types and specific brand-name models on the market. All cutting techniques are detailed, including compound and bevel sawing, making inlays, reliefs, and recesses, cutting metals and other nonwoods, and marquetry. There's even a section on transferring patterns to wood. Over 500 illustrations. 256 pages.

Scroll Saw Holiday Patterns. Patrick and Patricia Spielman provide over 100 full-size, shaded patterns for easy cutting, plus full-color photos of projects. Will serve all your holiday pleasures—all year long. Use these holiday patterns to create decorations, centerpieces, mailboxes, and diverse projects to keep or give as gifts. Standard holidays, as well as the four seasons, birthdays, and anniversaries, are represented. 8 pages of color. 168 pages.

Scroll Saw Pattern Book. The original classic pattern book—with over 450 patterns for wall plaques, refrigerator magnets, candle holders, pegboards, jewelry, ornaments, shelves, brackets, picture frames, signboards, and many other projects. Beginning and experienced scroll saw users alike will find something to intrigue and challenge them. 256 pages.

Scroll Saw Patterns for the Country Home. Patrick and Patricia Spielman and Sherri Spielman Valitchka produce a wide-ranging collection of over 200 patterns on country themes, including simple cutouts, mobiles, shelves, sculpture, pull toys, door and window toppers, clock holders, photo frames, layered pictures, and more. Over

80 black-and-white photos and 8 pages of color photos help you to visualize the steps involved as well as the finished projects. General instructions in Spielman's clear and concise style are included. 200 pages.

Scroll Saw Puzzle Patterns. 80 full-size patterns for jigsaw puzzles, stand-up puzzles, and inlay puzzles. With meticulous attention to detail, Patrick and Patricia Spielman provide instructions and step-by-step photos, along with tips on tools and wood selection, for making dinosaurs, camels, hippopotami, alligators—even a family of elephants! Inlay puzzle patterns include basic shapes, numbers, an accurate piece-together map of the United States, and a host of other colorful educational and enjoyable games for children. 8 pages of color. 264 pages.

Scroll Saw Shelf Patterns. Spielman and master scroll saw designer Loren Raty offer full-size patterns for 44 different shelf styles. Designs include wall shelves, corner shelves, and multi-tiered shelves. The patterns work well with ¼-inch hardwood, plywood, or any solid wood. Over 150 illustrations. 4 pages in color. 132 pages.

Scroll Saw Silhouette Patterns. With over 120 designs, Spielman and James Reidle provide an extremely diverse collection of intricate silhouette patterns, ranging from Victorian themes to sports to cowboys. They also include mammals, birds, country and nautical designs, as well as dragons, cars, and Christmas themes. Tips, hints, and advice are included along with detailed photos of finished works. 160 pages.

Sharpening Basics. The ultimate handbook, which goes well beyond the "basics" to become the major up-to-date reference work, features more than 300 detailed illustrations (mostly photos) explaining every facet of tool sharpening. Sections include bench-sharpening tools, sharpening machines, and safety. Chapters cover cleaning tools, and sharpening all sorts of tools, including chisels, plane blades (irons), hand knives, carving tools, turning tools, drill and boring tools, router and shaper tools, jointer and planer knives, drivers and scrapers, and, of course, saws. 128 pages.

Spielman's Original Scroll Saw Patterns. 262 full-size patterns that don't appear elsewhere feature teddy bears, dinosaurs, sports figures, dancers, cowboy cutouts, Christmas ornaments, and dozens more. Fretwork patterns are included for a Viking ship, framed cutouts, wall hangers, key-chain miniatures, jewelry, and much more. Hundreds of step-by-step photos and drawings show how to turn, repeat, and crop each design for thousands of variations. 4 pages of color. 228 pages.

Victorian Gingerbread: Patterns & Techniques. Authentic pattern designs (many full-size) cover the full range of indoor and outdoor detailing: brackets, corbels, shelves, grilles, spandrels, balusters, running trim, headers, valances, gable ornaments, screen doors, pickets, trellises, and much more. Also included are complete plans for Victorian mailboxes, house numbers, signs, and more. With clear instructions and helpful drawings by James Reidle, the book also provides tips for making gingerbread trim. 8 pages in color. 200 pages.

Victorian Scroll Saw Patterns. Intricate original designs plus classics from the 19th century are presented in full-size, shaded patterns. Instructions are provided with drawings and photos. Projects include alphabets and numbers, as well as silhouettes and designs for shelves, frames, filigree baskets, plant holders, decorative boxes, picture frames, welcome signs, architectural ornaments, and much more. 160 pages.

Woodworker's Pattern Library: Sports Figures. Spielman and Brian Dahlen have put together a full range of sports-related patterns for the new series *The Woodworker's Pattern Library*. Sports images for scroll-sawing enthusiasts include over 125 patterns in 34 categories of sporting activity. The patterns can be incorporated into functional projects such as signs or furniture and shelves or they can be used simply for decorative accent such as silhouettes in windows or against walls. An introductory section on Basic Tips provides information on enlarging and transferring patterns as well as cutting techniques such as stack-sawing. 128 pages.

Working Green Wood with PEG. Covers every process for making beautiful, inexpensive projects from green wood without cracking, splitting, or warping it. Hundreds of clear photos and drawings show every step from obtaining the raw wood through shaping, treating, and finishing PEG-treated projects. 175 unusual project ideas. Lists supply sources. 120 pages.

Index